The Adventure

The Adventure

GIORGIO AGAMBEN

TRANSLATED BY LORENZO CHIESA

THE MIT PRESS
CAMBRIDGE, MASSACHUSETTS
LONDON, ENGLAND

© 2018 Massachusetts Institute of Technology

Originally published as *L'avventura*. © 2015 nottetempo srl

All rights reserved. No part of this book may be reproduced in any form by any electronic or mechanical means (including photocopying, recording, or information storage and retrieval) without permission in writing from the publisher.

This book was set in Arnhem Pro by The MIT Press. Printed and bound in the United States of America.

Cover image: Christian Jank (1833–88), *The Garden of the Magician Klingsor*, from *The Parzival Cycle*, Great Music Room, ca. 1883–84 (mural) / Schloss Neuschwanstein, Bavaria, Germany / De Agostini Picture Library / A. Dagli Orti / Bridgeman Images

Library of Congress Cataloging-in-Publication Data

Names: Agamben, Giorgio, 1942– author.
Title: The adventure / Giorgio Agamben ; translated by Lorenzo Chiesa.
Other titles: Avventura. English
Description: Cambridge, MA : MIT Press, 2018. | Includes bibliographical references.
Identifiers: LCCN 2017028335 | ISBN 9780262037594 (hardcover : alk. paper)
Subjects: LCSH: Adventure and adventurers—Philosophy.
Classification: LCC G522 .A43 2018 | DDC 904—dc23 LC record available at https://lccn.loc.gov/2017028335

10 9 8 7 6 5 4 3 2 1

Contents

TRANSLATOR'S NOTE vii

1 DEMON 3
2 *AVENTURE* 27
3 EROS 49
4 EVENT 59
5 ELPIS 97

BIBLIOGRAPHY 103

TRANSLATOR'S NOTE

....

In line with my translations of Agamben's *The Fire and the Tale* (Stanford University Press, 2017) and *What Is Philosophy?* (Stanford University Press, 2017), as well as Adam Kotsko's translation of *The Use of Bodies* (Stanford University Press, 2015), I have here rendered the verb *esigere* as "to demand." The reader should bear in mind, however, that *esigere* also overlaps with "to require," "to call for," and "to necessitate."

Parola is translated as "speech" or "word," depending on the context.

I have rendered *potenza* as "power," where the term is not used in a technical manner, or "potency," where it presupposes the Aristotelian notion of *dynamis*. Following several English translations of Aristotle, I think "potency" conveys *dynamis/potenza* more effectively than "potentiality" (which is often preferred by Agamben's translators).

Given its proximity to *avventura* ("adventure"), the verb *avvenire* is crucial. For lack of a better term, I have translated it as "to happen," indicating the Italian original in brackets wherever Agamben's argument explicitly relies on both *avventura* and *avvenire*.

Where necessary, quotations have been modified to fit the Italian translations used by Agamben. Existing English translations have been consulted and incorporated as far as possible. Full bibliographical references are provided only when Agamben himself provides them.

I would like to thank Michael Lewis for his suggestions on how to render the passages on Heidegger in a way that is both faithful to Agamben's original and consonant with existing English translations.

The Adventure

1
Demon

> IN THE ASCENT TO HEAVEN,
> WHO CAN HAVE CONFIDENCE IN BEING ABLE
> TO MASTER THE FIVE-IN-HAND OF
> DAIMON, TYCHE, EROS, ANANKE, AND ELPIS?
> —ABY WARBURG

In Macrobius's *Saturnalia*, one of the characters participating in the symposium attributes to the Egyptians the belief that four deities preside over the birth of every human being: Daimon, Tyche, Eros, and Ananke (Demon, Chance, Love, and Necessity). "The Egyptians also use the caduceus's significance to explain the generation of people, which is called *genesis*, saying that four gods attend a human being as it is born: Demon, Chance, Love, and Necessity. The first two they mean to be regarded as the sun and the moon, because the sun as the source of spirit, warmth, and light, is the begetter and guardian of human life and so is believed to be the Daimon, or deity, of the one being born; whereas the moon is Tyche, because she is in charge of our bodies, which are buffeted by various chance circumstances. Love is signified by a Kiss, Necessity by a Knot" (*Saturnalia*, Bk. 1, chap. 19).

The life of every human being must pay tribute to these four deities, and should not try to elude or dupe them. Daimon must be honored because we owe him our character and nature; Eros because fecundity and knowledge depend on him; Tyche and Ananke because the art of living also involves a reasonable degree of bowing to what we cannot avoid. The way in which each person relates to these powers defines his or her ethics.

In 1817, Goethe comes across Macrobius's passage by chance while he is reading the work of a Danish philologist, Georg Zoëga, titled *Tyche and Nemesis*. In October of the same year, Goethe writes the *Urworte*, the "primal Words," where, reflecting on his life—he is sixty-eight by then—he tries in his way to pay his debt to Macrobius's deities, to which he adds Elpis, or Hope. More than anything else, these five short "orphic" stanzas (*Urworte: Orphisch* is the complete title) and the brief comments in prose that accompany them betray the superstition to which Goethe devoted his life, namely, the cult of the demon. A few years earlier, in a well-known passage of *Truth and Poetry*, he had already described his ambiguous relation with this unconceivable power:

> He believed that he perceived something in nature (whether living or lifeless, animate or inanimate) that manifested itself only in contradictions and therefore could not be expressed in any concept, much less in any word. It was not divine, for it seemed irrational; not human, for it had no intelligence; not diabolical, for it was beneficent; and not angelic, for it often betrayed malice. It was like chance, for it lacked continuity, and like Providence, for it suggested context. Everything that limits us seemed penetrable by it, and it appeared to do as it pleased with the

elements necessary to our existence, to contract time and expand space. It seemed only to accept the impossible and scornfully to reject the possible. This essence, which appeared to infiltrate all the others, separating and combining them, I called "daemonic," after the example of the ancients and others who had perceived something similar. I tried to save myself from this fearful thing.

Even a cursory reading of the *Urworte* shows that this devotion, which Goethe expressed with some reservations in his autobiography, is here organized as a sort of Creed, where astrology and science merge. For the poet, what was at stake in the demon was the attempt to turn the nexus of his life and work into a destiny. The Daimon that opens the list is in fact no longer an unconceivable and contradictory being, but, as witnessed by the addition of the orphic stanzas to his *The Metamorphosis of Plants*, has become a cosmic power and a kind of law of nature:

> As the sun was placed greeting
>   the planets
> the day that lent you to the world,
> you began to grow and thrive
> according to the law, which made
>   you appear.
> That way you must be, you cannot
>   escape yourself,
> Sibyls and Prophets revealed it
>   long ago.
> No power and no time is able to
>   destroy

such imprinted form, which develops while living.

In the prose commentary, Goethe emphatically adds: "Demon means here the necessary and limited individuality immediately expressed at birth ... the innate force and property that more than anything else rules over the destiny of mankind." Just as in his autobiography chance was nothing other than an aspect of the demonic, so here the orphic word that follows—Tyche, the Fortuitous (*das Zufällige*)—is only the ever-changing element that, especially among young people, accompanies and distracts "with its inclinations and games" the demon who at each turn manages to preserve himself through them. Bringing together the demon and chance in a personal destiny, Goethe gave expression to his most secret belief.

Coming to terms with Eros is more complicated, since, with respect to this third deity, Goethe certainly could not ignore that he failed to obey him. The "erotic indecision" and "omission" Benjamin reproaches him with in his article for the *Great Soviet Encyclopedia* and his essay titled *Elective Affinities* actually amounted to a renunciation of perseverance in love relationships. It is significant that the only relationship Goethe did not end was that with Christiane Vulpius, a worker in an artificial flower factory with whom he had a son and whom he decided to marry after fifteen years, precisely because the unbridgeable social difference that separated them prevented him from seeing in marriage anything other than a compensation owed to the mother of his only son. It is therefore unsurprising that, in *Orphic Words*, Eros appears in a distinctly unfavorable light. As explained in the prose commentary, in love, the individual demon lets himself being seduced by "Tyche the temptress," and, "while he seems to be obeying only himself and leave the field open to his will," he actually submits to "randomness and extraneous elements that distance him from his path: he believes he is seizing something, but in truth he imprisons himself; he believes he is winning but instead he is defeated."

In Macrobius's last and dark deity—Ananke, or Necessity—Goethe sees the power that, against Tyche and Eros's deviations, tightens the fateful link between the individual and his demon. In this sense, she gives a name to the same astral force of the "law" (*Gesetz*) that already defined the demon in the first stanza:

> Then it is again as the stars wished:
> condition and law; all will
> is only wishing because we simply
>   should,
> and before the will freedom is silent;
> the most beloved thing is chided away
>   by the heart,
> to the hard "must" comply will
>   and whim.
> So we are free from semblances, after
>   many years
> just closer to where we were in the
>   beginning.

In *Orphic Words* Goethe really paid his tribute to only one deity: the Daimon. This choice also clarifies the poet's guiding strategy; inscribing his own existence into a demonic constellation, he intended to distance it from every ethical judgment. *Orphic Words* thus seals the declaration of nonresponsibility that the poet professed in the fragment *On Nature* when he was thirty: "She has brought me here, she will lead me away. I trust myself to her. She may do as she will with me. She will not hate her work. ... Hers is the blame, hers the glory." But, since responsibility is a juridical and not an ethical concept, the gesture that claims to dismiss it is as alien to ethics as that which would like to assume it. This gesture rather betrays distress, and the poet could not have been unaware of it. The demon with whom Goethe made an informal deal, one that is yet no less firm than Faust's, is the ambiguous power that guarantees success to the individual on condition of renouncing every ethical decision. It is thanks to this pact that Goethe could fashion his life as if the most insignificant episode or the most casual maxim showed the demonic signature that sanctioned its inevitable outcome, which a flock of scribes and assistants (Eckermann, Riemer, Müller) had to register. Life and writing, which the demon had combined into a destiny, were reciprocally the sufficient guarantee of their success.

Perhaps it is because of his awareness of this flight from responsibility that Goethe had to add a fifth divine name to the four listed by Macrobius, one for which he stated he was anticipating an "ethical and religious" commentary. Elpis, or Hope, which closes the prosimetrum, is here nothing other than Daimon in disguise, who, with her wing-beat, should raise the life of the individual beyond the Earth and time ("A wing-beat—and behind us aeons"). This last orphic word lacks faith, which, following Saint Paul's postulate, alone could give it some substance ("Hope that is seen is no hope at all"—Romans 8:25; "Faith is the substance of what we hope for"—Hebrews 11:1). Elpis remains imprisoned in the superstitious sphere of the demon. The poet expects to be saved by the demon, not hope. But claiming to arrange the shapeless chaos of our life into a demonic order that unfailingly leads it to success is necessarily superstitious; on the contrary, authentic piety is recognizing precisely in the sober acceptation of that chaos the only precondition for searching for a way out of every apparent order.

Mentioning Tyche among the deities that protect and direct the life of humankind, Macrobius was referring to a tradition that, starting already in the fourth century BC, granted her an eminent rank (it is significant that Oedipus defines himself as "son of Tyche"—*Oedipus Rex*, l. 1080). In a passage from Dio Chrysostom, which Macrobius might have known, Tyche's eminence is translated into an unexpected expansion of her skills, which leads her to assume those traditionally reserved to other—and apparently more powerful—deities. Dio writes: "Tyche has been given many names among men. Her impartiality [*to ison*] has been named Nemesis; her invisibility [*to adelon*],

Elpis; her inevitability, Moira; her righteousness, Themis—truly a deity of many names and many ways" (*Discourses*, 64, 8).

It is no coincidence that among Tyche's names listed here are those of at least two deities from the *Urworte*: Elpis, or Hope, and Ananke (Moira, or Destiny, is the daughter of Necessity). But also behind the gloomy mask of Nemesis (from *nemein*, to assign, "the one who assigns") it is possible to recognize the youthful face of Daimon (*daimon*, from *daiomai*, literally means "the one who apportions and assigns the character of every person"). Tyche is not only chance; no matter how contradictory this may seem to us, she is also destiny and necessity. Tyche is truly the power "of many names," which governs the paths and fate of humankind in every field.

One of Hippocrates's well-known aphorisms summarizes medical art by articulating five terms: "Life [*bios*] is short, art [*techne*] is long, occasion [*kairos*] is fleeting [*oxys*: "sharp," "difficult to seize"], experience [*peira*] is deceiving, and judgment [*krisis*] is difficult."

A secret connection unites this draconian list, in which the brief adventure of human life is at stake, with the five quasi deities of Macrobius and Goethe. *Kairos* and *krisis*, the moment of judgment in which the doctor needs to decide whether the patient will survive, evoke the most obscure part of Daimon and Tyche. And in experience—but *peira* also means "endeavor," "to prove oneself"—Necessity and Hope seem to combine for a moment through a peripeteia, whose outcome is inseparable from the possibility of deceit and illusion.

2
Aventure

> "IS IT THOU, THEN, O DAME ADVENTURE?"
> —WOLFRAM VON ESCHENBACH

In the prologue to one of Chrétien de Troyes's most astonishing poems of chivalry, *Yvain*, the protagonist introduces himself as follows:

> "Je sui," fet il, "uns chevaliers
> qui quier ce que trover ne puis;
> assez ai quis, et rien ne truis."
> "Et que voldroies tu trover?"
> "Aventure, por esprover

> ma proesce et mon hardement.
> Or te pri et quier et demant,
> se tu sez, que tu me consoille
> ou d'aventure ou de mervoille."
> "A ce," fet il, "faudras tu bien:
> d'aventure ne sai je rien
> n'oncques mes n'en oï parler."

> "I am," he said, "a knight
> seeking what I cannot find;
> long have I sought and nothing I have found."
> "And what is this thou fain wouldst find?"
> "Some adventure whereby to test
> my prowess and my bravery.
> Now I beg and urgently request thee
> to give me some counsel, if possible,

concerning some adventure or
   marvelous thing."
Says he: "Thou only can do it,
for I know nothing of adventure,
nor did I ever hear tell of such."
(*Yvain*, ll. 358–369)

The term *aventure* with which the knight defines the object of his search—and, through it, even himself—was possibly not immediately clear, if his interlocutor can candidly admit he never heard of it. The only certain thing is that it has to do with marvel (*d'aventure ou de mervoille*) and that it will function as a test for Yvain's bravery. We cannot understand the semantic subtlety of this passage unless we recall that the Old French verb *trover* does not simply mean "to find." Although philologists do not agree on its etymology, it is certain that it was originally a technical term of the Romance poetological vocabulary, whose meaning was "to compose poetry" (this is why poets called themselves *trobadors*, *trouvères*, or *trovatori*).

Yvain, who is seeking what he cannot find, could then be a figure for Chrétien who "finds" the topic of his poem: the knight's adventure is the same as the poet's.

An investigation of the possible etymology of the term *aventure* should begin by calling into question Meyer-Lübke's simplistic hypothesis, which traces it back to the supposed Latin **adventura*. Not only is the term not attested in classical Latin, but the oft-repeated interpretation—which sees in the term the plural neutral of the future participle of *advenio*—has no rational basis, at least since it has been demonstrated that Latin nouns ending in *-ura* do not necessarily derive from the future participle.

Whether it derives from the classical and Christian Latin *adventus* (the advent of a prince or a messiah), as is likely, or from *eventus*, as the late Du Cange suggested, the term designates something mysterious or marvelous that happens to a given man, which could be equally positive or negative. In this sense, the connection with *advena* and *adventicius*—two terms that designate the stranger—is significant. In any case, as Eberwein observed, what is decisive is "the moment of an effective occurrence within a real and known context" (Eberwein, 32).

For this reason, in chivalric poems, *Aventure* seems to have as many meanings as Tyche.

Like Tyche, it designates both chance and destiny: the unexpected event that challenges the knight and a series of facts that will necessarily take place. The adverbial expression *par aventure*, "by chance," and the adjective *aventureux*, in the sense of "risky" (*la lande aventureuse / et la rivière perilleuse—Guingamor*, ll. 357–358[1]), derive from the first meaning. The multiple connotations of the term, in the sense of "providential event" or "good fortune," "ill fate" or "misfortune" (*sventura*), derive from the second. However, what is crucial is the irresistible involvement of the subject in the adventure that happens to him. As suggested (by Ranke et al., 16–29), adventure is for the knight an encounter with both the world and himself, and for this reason, a source of desire and awe at the

---

1. "The adventurous land / and the perilous river"—Trans.

same time. In one of Marie de France's *lais*, after meeting his beloved, the protagonist returns home so distressed that he doubts himself and what he saw:

> De s'aventure vait pensant
> e en sun curage dotant
> esbaïz est, ne seit que creir[e]
> il ne la quide mie a veir[e].

> Thinking of his adventure, he goes
> along; doubts fill his heart; he knows
> not what to believe; dazzled he
> can't believe that it's the truth.
> (*Lanval*, ll. 197–200)

And yet, the stranger and riskier the adventure, the more desirable it becomes:

> Mes con plus granz est la mervoille
> et l'aventure plus grevainne,
> plus le covoite et plus se painne.
>
> But the greater the wonder
> and the more perilous the adventure,
> the more he covets it and yearns for it.
> (*Erec et Enide*, ll. 5644–5646)

Jacob Grimm—the ingenious coauthor of *Kinder- und Hausmärchen*—was the first to comment on the double meaning of the Old German term *âventiure* and the Old French *aventure*, from which it derives. "In addition to event [*Ereignis*] and occurrence, *âventiure* also means tale [*Erzählung*], or description, just as 'story' [*Geschichte*] designates not only what happened [*das Geschehene*] but also its narration [*Bericht*]" (Grimm, 6). The *aventure* (or *âventiure*) may be marvelous or fortuitous (in which case it means "chance"), beneficial or malefic (one will then call it *bonne* or *male aventure*; the term seems to be equivalent to "fate" or "fortune"), or more or less perilous (it will thus stand as a challenge to the knight's courage); however, it is not always easy to distinguish between the event and its transposition into words. This difficulty is witnessed by the incipit of many texts, both Old French and Old German: *Ici commence l'aventure ...*; *Als uns diu âventiure zalt ...*; or, in *Parzival*, the statement that "Flegetanis wrote the Grail adventure" (*Flegetânis schreip von grâles âventiur*—*Parzival*, 453, l. 30). What begins or is written is first and foremost the story, but this fully coincides with the protagonist's adventurous vicissitudes.

This is why, like a book or a living being, the adventure has a name, which is "very fair to say": "L'aventure, ce vos plevis, / La Joie de la Cort a non" (*Erec et Enide*, ll. 5464–5465).[2]

It is precisely this connection that turned "destiny" into one of the possible meanings of the term "adventure"; in fact, destiny is nothing other than a series of events that are said or predicted by an authoritative speech. A short Old French poem states that the God Apollo

> Bien dit a chascun s'aventure,
> mes sa responsse est mout obscure.
>
> Well says everybody's adventure
> but his response is very obscure.
> (*Roman de Thèbes*, ll. 191–192)

---

2. "The adventure, upon my word, is called 'the Joy of the Court'"—Trans.

AVENTURE

On the other hand,

Aventure qui estre dit
ne poet remaindre qu'el ne seit,
e chose qui deit avenir
ne poet por nule chose faillir.

An adventure that has to take place
cannot be prevented,
and something that has to happen
cannot fail to do so for any reason.
(*Roman de Rou*, ll. 5609–5612)

Adventure and speech, life and language merge, and the metal that results from their fusion is that of destiny.

A contemporary of Chrétien, Marie de France turns the word *aventure* into a technical term par excellence of her poetics. In this way, it preserves all the semantic richness and ambiguity described by Grimm. However, we need to leave aside the *lectio facilior* according to which adventure is only the narrative content of the *lai*, that is, the story it tells. If, following Spitzer, we in fact understand the specific temporal framework that Marie creates for her *lais*, we also realize that the adventure does not precede the story as a chronological event but remains inseparable from it from the beginning. Undoubtedly, in the prologue the poet states that she is transcribing and putting into rhymes the *lais* she has heard, which were composed "to remember" (*pur remembrance*) adventures; but—as is clearly said in *Guigemar*—these "adventures" are always already "stories," or rather are always already written:

AVENTURE

> Les contes ke jo sai verrais,
> dunt li Bretun unt fait les lais,
> vos conterai assez briefment.
> El chief de cest comencement,
> sulunc la lettre et l'escriture
> vos mosterai une aventure.
>
> The stories that I know to be true,
> whereof the Britons have made lais,
> I will tell you shortly.
> And in the beginning,
> according to the letter and the writing
> I will set before you an adventure.
> (*Guigemar*, ll. 19–24)

Like Warburg's *Pathosformel*, adventure is the timeless crystal that holds together the chain of memory in which Marie inserts her *lais*: in *remembrance*, event and tale coincide.

In this sense, adventure is always *l'aventure d'un lai*: *L'aventure d'un autre lai / cum ele avient, vus cunterai* ("The adventure of another lai, / just as it happened, I'll relay"—*Lanval*, ll. 1–2).

Marie can tell the adventure immediately as it happens (unlike *coment*, *cum* has a temporal value in the *lais*) because it is not an event located in a chronological past, but is always already an event of speech.

Marie de France hints at the truth of what she is telling several times, but she does it in a way that seems to blend truth and adventure. For instance, *Eliduc* literally resumes the formula quoted from *Lanval*, yet replaces *aventure* with *verité*: "Just as it happened I will relay / I will tell its truth" (*Si cum avient vus cunterai, / la verité vus en dirrai*—*Eliduc*, ll. 27–28).

AVENTURE

In the conclusion of *Chevrefoil*, the poet claims she has told "the *lai*'s truth," just as elsewhere she said she told its adventure: "I've spoken for you the truth / of the *lai* which I relayed for you today" (*Dit vus en ai la verité / del lai que j'ai ici cunté*—*Chevrefoil*, ll. 117–118).

The truth in question here is neither the apophantic truth of logic nor historical truth. It is poetic truth. That is to say, it is not a correspondence between events and tale, facts and words; rather it is their coincidence in the adventure. We are not dealing with two things: the adventure-event and the adventure-tale, where the latter is true if it faithfully reproduces the former and false if it does not. Adventure and truth are indiscernible, because truth happens (*avviene*) and adventure is nothing other than the happening (*avvenire*) of truth.

In the poetry of the Minnesänger, adventure is personified by a woman and becomes *Frau Âventiure*. In Wolfram von Eschenbach's *Parzival*, she appears suddenly to the poet and asks him to let her enter into his heart:

> "Tout ûf!" "Wem? Wer sît ir?"
> "Ich wil inz herze hin zuo dir."
> "Sô gert ir zengem rûme."
> "Waz denne, belîbe ich kûme?
> Mîn dringen soltu selten klagen,
> ich wil dir nu von wunder sagen."
> "Jâ sît irz, Frau Âventiure?"
>
> "Open!" "To whom? Who art thou?"
> "In thine heart would I find a place."

"Too narrow shall be the space."
"What of that? Even
if too narrow shall be the space,
thou shalt not bewail my coming.
Such marvels I'll tell to thee."
"Is it thou, then, O Dame Adventure?"
(*Parzival*, 433, ll. 1–8)

Although, in both Wolfram's poem and later texts, we are always presented with an actual creature, *Frau Âventiure* is also undoubtedly the very story that is being told. When speaking to her, Wolfram is addressing the very tale he is writing. This is why, in Ulrich von Liechtenstein's *Frauendienst*, *Âventiure* knocks at the poet's door not with her fist but with words ("Open! I'm knocking with words, let me in"—*Frauendienst*, l. 515); in Rudolf von Ems's *Wilhelm von Orlens*, she even introduces herself by asking: "Who has read me?" (*Wer hât mich guoter her gelesen?*—*Wilhelm von Orlens*, l. 2143). The very act of writing and narrating is embodied in Dame Adventure; but insofar as it coincides with the narrated events, this act is not a book but the living body of a woman. Wolfram's enigmatic statement—"It is not a book [*buoch*]: I know no letter [*ine kan decheinen buochstap*]" (*Parzival*, 115, l. 27)—becomes on this perspective perfectly comprehensible. Contrary to what some interpreters believe, this is not a declaration of ignorance, but rather the awareness that adventure is situated not merely in a text or in a series of events, but in their coincidence—that is, in their falling together.

As Grimm did not fail to notice, insofar as it is a "personification of the narrated story,"

AVENTURE 37

there is not just one Dame Adventure, but "as many particular Âventiure as there are individual tales" (Grimm, 22). And each adventure searches for "a Meister who turns it into a poem and to whom she may reveal all her secrets" (ibid.).

It is this indetermination of event and speech in *Frau Âventiure* that can somehow shed light on the details of another episode from *Parzival*, which interpreters have always deemed obscure. The young hero, deranged and inexperienced, arrives at one point in a field close to the forest of Brizljan and sees a woman sleeping in a tent.

> Diu frouwe was entslâfen.
> Si trouc der minne wâfen,
> einen munt durchliuhtic rôt,

und gerndes ritters herzen nôt.
Innen des diu frouwe slief,
der munt ir von einander lief:
der trouc der minne hitze fiur.

The woman slumbered.
Yet weapons of love she bore:
a mouth so red and glowing,
that the knight's heart had
    wounded sore.
And as she slept
they parted asunder,
her lips so bright,
that the fire of love had kindled.
(*Parzival*, 130, ll. 3–9)

The peculiarity is that the term adventure, which appears at this point, does not refer to Parzival's experience, but to the sleeping woman: "Thus lay the marvelous adventure" (*Sus lac des wunsches âventiur*—ibid., 130, l. 10). Wolfram can here call the woman "adventure" because her body is the cipher of both the adventure that Parzival is living and the tale the poet is narrating. Meeting the woman named Jeschûte, Parzival meets his own story.

Grimm traces the genealogy of *Frau Âventiure* back to the personification of poetic inspiration as a goddess that is present in both the classical tradition (the "Muse") and the Germanic one (in *Edda*, the Saga is defined as a goddess, *asynja*). "The German concept that lay behind it is thus transferred from a Saga that speaks and tells to what is spoken and told. 'Saga' itself designated the event insofar as it was told and not insofar as it happened.

Wolfram did not invent anything new or unknown; he only gave it a foreign name, which determined and limited it" (Grimm, 22). But in this way Grimm overlooks the particular signature that defines the adventure. As Grimm cannot fail to notice, an indicator of this difference is that the meeting with *Frau Âventiure* does not happen (*avviene*) at the beginning of the poem but in the course of narration, and therefore, unlike in the classical tradition, it never has the form of an invocation.

Âventiure appears in the middle of the story because, unlike the Muse, she is not the numinous power that preexists the tale and makes the poet speak; rather, she is the tale and lives only in and through it. Here, the woman is not the one who inspires the poet to speak; she is the very event of speech—she is not the gift of the tale but the tale itself.

Aventure (*âventiure*) is an essential technical term of the medieval poetic vocabulary. It has been recognized as such by modern scholars, who stress the poetological meaning the term acquires in Hartmann von Aue (but it was already implicit in Chrétien de Troyes—see Mertens, 339), as well as the performative character the poetic text acquires to the extent that the act of telling and the content of the tale tend to converge (see Strohschneider, 379–380).

However, we are also interested here in another aspect of the adventure. Insofar as it expresses the inseparable unity of event and tale, thing and speech, the adventure cannot but have a properly ontological meaning beyond its poetological value. If being is the dimension opened to humans in the anthropogenetic event of language; if being is always, in Aristotle's words, something that "is said," then the adventure certainly deals with a specific experience of being.

3
Eros

ARTURI REGIS AMBAGES PULCERRIME.
—DANTE ALIGHIERI

Before trying to define this experience of being, we need to dismiss the modern conceptions of adventure, which run the risk of obstructing our access to the original meaning of the term. The end of the Middle Ages and the beginning of the modern age in fact coincide with an obscuration and devaluation of adventure. In their dictionary, the Brothers Grimm quote a significant example of the pejorative use of the term in Luther, who, speaking about the effectiveness of baptism, states: "Baptism does not amount to an event, this is an adventure" (*Die taufe steht nicht auf eventum, das ist ebenthewr*). But it is in Hegel that the condemnation of adventure is unreservedly sanctioned. In the chapter titled "Adventures" of the section of *Lectures on Aesthetics* devoted to the "Romantic Form of Art," Hegel targets chivalric romance and medieval poetry in general. Adventure is defined by the fact that, in it, the mind refers to the external world "not as to its own reality permeated by itself, but as to something purely external separated from it," which, precisely for this reason, "unfolds by itself, complicates itself, and moves like an endlessly flowing, mutable, and confusing contingency" (Hegel, 586). By introducing "accidental collisions" and "extraordinarily intertwined ramifications," this exteriority and contingency of the ends with respect to the subject who pursues them constitute "adventure, which provides for the form of events and actions the fundamental type of the romantic" (ibid., 587). Hegel refers to the "search for the Holy Grail" (ibid., 589) and—oddly enough—Dante's *Divine Comedy* as examples of this accidental character of medieval adventure. The same contingency and exteriority can also be found in the close link that seems to connect adventure with love in medieval literature: "So here the actions on behalf of love, e.g. in their more detailed character, have in them, in great part, no other determining factor save affording proofs of firmness, fidelity, and constancy in love, and showing that the surrounding reality with the whole complex of its relationships counts only as material for the manifestation of love. Thereby the specific act of this manifestation, since it is only the proof [of love] that matters, is not determined by itself but is left to the fancy or mood of the lady and to the caprice of external contingencies" (ibid., 589–590). According to Hegel, it is precisely because the amorous adventure of chivalry remains external to the subject that, with Ariosto and Cervantes, it inevitably ends up leading to the dissolution of the romantic form of art it embodies: "Carried through consistently, this whole field of adventurousness [*Abenteuerei*] proves in its actions and events, as well as in their outcomes, to be an inherently self-dissolving and therefore comical world of incidents and fates (ibid., 590–591).

It is difficult to imagine a more complete misunderstanding of the medieval intention: as we saw, not only does adventure never remain external to the knight who is living it, but, even with respect to the poet, it turns out to be so far from contingent that, as *Frau Âventiure*, it instead penetrates his heart and is identified with the very text he is writing.

The idea that adventure is something external—and therefore eccentric and bizarre—with respect to ordinary life defines its modern conception. It is present even in the otherwise incisive essay Simmel devotes to this theme. Starting from the first page, Simmel writes that "the most general form of adventure is its dropping out of the continuity of life." This is why it is compared with dreams, which are located outside of the signifying connections that characterize the "wholeness of life" (Simmel, 222). However, Simmel realizes that, although adventure unfolds outside the continuity of life, "it is distinct from all that is accidental and alien," since it does not merely touch life's outer shell but is "somehow connected with [its] centre" (ibid.). In this way it is similar to the work of art, which cuts out a piece of the infinite series of experiences and bestows upon it an autonomous form; although it is only a part of individual existence, adventure is "nevertheless felt as a whole, as an integrated unit" (ibid., 223). In other words, the concept of adventure is defined by the fact that something isolated and accidental contains meaning and necessity, and "despite its accidental nature, its extraterritoriality with respect to the continuity of life, it nevertheless connects with the character and destiny of the bearer of that life … in the widest sense, transcending, by a mysterious necessity, life's more narrowly rational aspects" (ibid., 224).

Here Simmel seems to acknowledge the insufficiency of a (modern) conception of adventure that places it outside of the context of common existence. Although he refers only to Casanova and the gambler as examples of adventurers, in one passage of the essay Simmel somehow comes close to the medieval experience and evokes the possibility that "life as a whole may be perceived as an adventure" (ibid., 225). "For this, one need neither be an adventurer nor undergo many adventures. To have such a remarkable attitude toward life, one must sense above its totality a higher unity, a super-life, as it were, whose relation to life parallels the relation of the immediate life totality itself to those particular experiences which we call adventures" (ibid.).

Simmel is unable to unravel this twofold nature of adventure—its being only a part of existence and its bestowing upon it a superior unity. This is why adventure is, for him, essentially contradictory: it shows at the same time the characteristics of activity and passivity, certainty and uncertainty, whereby, on the one hand, it makes us take possession of the world violently and resolutely, and, on the other, it causes us to abandon ourselves to it with infinitely fewer defenses and reservations than in ordinary existence. "The unity toward which at every moment, by the very process of living, we bring together our activity and our passivity with regard to the world—the unity which even in a certain sense *is* life itself—accentuates its disparate elements most sharply ... as if they were only the two aspects of one and the same, mysteriously seamless life" (ibid., 226).

This is evident also in the constitutive link Simmel establishes between adventure and love. The link is so close that "our linguistic custom hardly lets us understand by 'adventure' anything but an erotic one" (ibid., 227). In fact, love presents the same twofold nature that defines adventure: love unites in itself "conquering force and unextortable concession, winning by one's own abilities and dependence on the luck which something incalculable outside ourselves bestows on us" (ibid.). These two poles of the erotic experience—conquest and grace—are closely linked in woman and more neatly opposed in man, so that their sudden coincidence in love confers upon it that character of adventure that, according to Simmel, is specifically masculine. But the connection between amorous experience and adventure is even more deep-seated. Just as adventure seems to transcend the unitary flow of life and, at the same time, be bound to "the most recondite instincts and some ultimate intention of life as a whole" (ibid., 228), so too does love live out of this interweaving of a tangential and momentary trait and something that lies at the center of human existence. "It may give to our life only a momentary splendour, like the ray shed in an inside room by a light flitting by outside. Still it satisfies a need … which—whether it be considered as physical, psychic, or metaphysical—exists, as it were, timelessly in the foundation or center of our being" (ibid.). It is precisely the relation with this deep-seated erotic center that bestows upon adventure its claim to totality and, at the same time, turns it into "a form which by its temporal symbolism seems to be predetermined to receive the erotic content" (ibid.).

At the end of the essay, Simmel defines humans as "adventurers of the earth" (ibid., 232) and seems to grasp that, in adventure, life goes beyond its material basis and episodes. However, adventure ultimately remains a "time stolen" from the process of events that constitute our existence. It is no coincidence that, in his reflection on adventure, Simmel did not take into consideration those poems of chivalry in which it had appeared for the first time in European literature. In them, for the individual to whom it happens (*a cui avviene*), adventure is in fact fully identified with life, not only because it affects and transfigures his whole existence, but also and above all because it transforms the subject himself, regenerating him as a new creature (who is conventionally called a "knight," but has nothing to do with the homonymous social figure). If Eros and adventure are here often intimately entwined, this is not because love gives meaning and legitimacy to adventure, but, on the contrary, because only a life that has the form of adventure can truly find love.

We owe to Oskar Becker, one of Heidegger's early students, an attempt to formulate a philosophical theory of adventure. In Heidegger's thought, human existence is defined by its potentiality-for-Being; however, the possibilities we are thus given are not empty but always "thrown" into one or another specific situation. The emotional mood in which man opens to the world discloses him as always already "consigned to that being which, in existing, he has to be" (Heidegger, *Being and Time*, 173), that is, as thrown into a situation he cannot escape but which yet remains impenetrable for him. This is why existence—*Dasein*—can at times be defined as a weight and a "burden" that we must shoulder.

Becker opposes this pathos of "being-thrown" to the lightness of being-carried (*Getragensein*), which defines the "adventurousness" of the artist's existence. The expression "being-carried" should not be taken literally, as if we were still confronted with a weight that must be borne. We must rather think of the peculiar weightless mobility of the firmament in the ancient conception of the celestial spheres. In other words, we are dealing with a being-carried devoid of anything that supports us, that is, a life experience in which what orients us is not the situation to which we are consigned or the task we need to assume, but an absolute lack of weight and task.

Becker calls "adventure" the condition of an existence—such as that of the artist—that is placed in between "the extreme insecurity of being-thrown and the absolute security of being-carried, between the extremely problematic character of what is historical and the absolute absence of problems that characterizes every natural being" (Becker, 31–32). In other words, it is a matter of interrogating "the aesthetic man's existence" and describing the "fruitful and perhaps even terrible moment" (ibid.) the artist experiences as he completes his work. He did not create it on the basis of a decision; the work gave itself to him and "carried" him until its completion. Becker writes that "the security of the genius has something of the sleepwalker; he is vigilant and enlightened by extreme clarity, yet not simply vigilant and sober but enraptured by divine *mania*."

It is significant here that the artist takes the place of the knight as the subject of the adventure. The existential condition of being-carried is so strictly modeled on that of aesthetic experience that it is difficult to avoid the impression that what is at stake for Becker is nothing other than the aestheticization of existence—which has its archetype in the German Romantics. It is therefore not surprising that what defines the artist's adventurousness is the concept of irony—so dear to the Romantics. "The artist devoted to the completion of his work is instantaneous and eternal; he is both things at the same time and knows he is this irreconcilability; along with it, he knows he is inessential, a pure phenomenon, a metaphysical adventurer unveiled as such; his being is at the same time semblance and truth: he is irony" (ibid., 35).

Nothing could be more distant from the adventure of the medieval knight, who not only does not know irony but can never conceive of adventure as an aestheticization of existence.

It is no coincidence that Becker's essay ends with a quotation from Goethe's *Urworte*, which exemplifies "the emotional mood of being-carried" with the demon (ibid., 42). Against Benjamin's warning—who recommends we not confuse life with work—what is again at stake is illegitimately uniting the work of art with the existence of its author.

A decisive objection against adventure was tacitly made at the end of the Middle Ages. It implicitly emerges from the peculiar fact that Dante never uses the term—except for two occurrences in *Vita Nuova* (XIV, 10) and *Convivio* (II, XI, 8), where it appears in the adverbial syntagm "per aventura"—although it was common in the language of his time; in the negative form "disaventura," it had even become a technical term of amorous experience in the poetry of his "first friend," Guido Cavalcanti ("my strong and new misadventure"—XXXIV, 1; "I fear that my misadventure"—XXXIII, 1; but also "How adventurous / my desire was"—I, 21–22).

The fact that the term—crucial to the chivalric tradition with which the love poets were so familiar—does not appear in the more than fifteen thousand verses of the *Divine Comedy* betrays something like a positive intention. For Dante, not only amorous experience but, more generally, our life on Earth—the sequence of events that leads us from sin and confusion to salvation—are not presented as an "adventure."

In *De vulgari eloquentia*, Dante uses a similar term when, mentioning the chivalric subject matters written in *langue d'oïl*, he evokes the *Arturi regis ambages pulcerimme* (I, X, 2). *Ambages*—which literally indicates a tortuous movement (*ambago*) or going around in circles—is a word Virgil uses, and, in the *Aeneid*, it has a clearly negative meaning (*longa est iniuria, longae / ambages*—I,

341–342; *horrendas canit ambages*—VI, 99; *dolos tecti ambagesque*—VI, 29—with reference to Daedalus's labyrinth[1]). In *Paradise* XVII, 31-33, it appears with the same negative meaning: "Né per ambage, in che la gente folle / già s'inviscava pria che fosse anciso / l'Agnel di Dio."[2] However, in *De vulgari*, the ambages—King Arthur and his knights' tortuous wanderings—are defined as "most beautiful." Thus, by subsequently refusing the term "adventure," Dante has in mind not simply a poetic judgment, but something that concerns the very conception of human life and therefore has both philosophical and theological implications.

---

1. "Long is the wrong, long the devious tales"; "[She] sang horrible riddles"; "The intricacies and winding alleys of the structure"—Trans.
2. "Nor with dark riddles such as the foolish folk of old were ensnared by before the Lamb of God was slain"—Trans.

In the letter to Can Grande, Dante describes the subject of his poem in the following terms: "The subject is man, as by either gaining or losing merit through his freedom of will, he is liable to rewarding or punishing justice" (*Epistola* XIII, 24). Shortly after he specifies that the kind of philosophy the poem belongs to is ethics (*morale negotium sive ethica*—ibid., 40). It is this conception of the human condition that determined Dante's separation from the "most beautiful ambages" of the Arthurian knights and his repudiation of adventure. The human vicissitude that is revealed to the poet "midway upon the journey of our life" is not an adventure and does not proceed in circles along most beautiful (though tortuous and endless) ambages—which as such are clearly located outside of ethics and the theological-juridical paradigm of punishment and reward, perdition and salvation. It proceeds in a straight line, from sin to redemption, without giving in to the uncertainties, fortuity, digressions, and tergiversations of chivalric adventure.

In this sense, amorous experience—starting at least from *Vita Nuova*—is itself distanced from the sphere of adventure. Certainly, like *Frau Âventiure*, Beatrice is an indiscernible product of poetry and life, tale and event, language and reality: however, she is never merely the protagonist or the goal of a marvelous or shady adventure who as such never fully steps out of the pages that describe her. Love is neither an adventure nor a misadventure—this is perhaps the difference between Dante's and Cavalcanti's conceptions of it; love is a redemptive experience, a path that slowly but steadily unfolds from obscurity to conscience, loss to redemption, and speech to what transcends it. The fact that Lancelot's name is briefly evoked precisely with regard to Paolo and Francesca's sin shows that if love remains imprisoned in the field of adventure and the book ("when we read ..."), it can only be lost.

In the letter to Can Grande, Dante also explains the title of the poem by saying that, while tragedy begins quietly and marvelously (*admirabilis*) but ends horribly, comedy begins with an "asperity" but ends happily. Human life is not an adventure; in this specific sense of the term, it is simply a comedy.

4
Event

> THE EVENT IS NOT WHAT HAPPENS.
> —GILLES DELEUZE

In 1952, Carlo Diano published the essay "Forma ed evento," possibly his most ambitious theoretical work, in *Giornale critico della filosofia italiana*. Here he opposes form—Plato and Aristotle's *eidos*—which is in itself accomplished and unchangeable outside of any relation, to the event, which is always inscribed into a relation and can never be substantivized into an essence (and which the Stoics turned into a central concept of their thought). What interests us is not the opposition and articulation of these two categories—which Diano employs for his interpretation of the Greek world—but rather his definition of the event, which he traces back to *tyche*. He notices that, deriving from the verb *tynchano* ("to happen"), the term *tyche* is formed out of the aorist tense and therefore refers to a temporary and undetermined happening—that is, in this sense, to the opposite of the *moira* and the *heimarmene*, which, being formed out of the perfect tense, indicate the necessity and immutability of what has been. In this sense, *tyche* is nothing other than "a hypostatization of the event" (Diano, 20)—not of the event in its indifferent randomness, but insofar as it happens to somebody. "The event is therefore not *quicquid evenit*, but *id quod cuique evenit*. ... This difference is crucial. The fact that it rains is something that happens, but this does not suffice to turn it into an event; for this to be an event it is necessary that I perceive such a happening as happening to me" (ibid., 72).

It is easy to recognize here the traits of the adventure, which always and immediately involves the knight who is living it. If, as *e-ventus*, it happens (*avviene*) instantaneously and we do not know where it comes from, as *ad-ventus* it always happens to and for somebody in a given place. As Diano writes, "the event is always *hic et nunc*. There is an event only in the precise place where I am and at the moment when I perceive it" (ibid., 74). By happening (*avvenendo*), the adventure demands "someone" to whom it happens (*a cui avvenire*). However, this does not mean that the event—the adventure—depends on the subject: "It is not the *hic et nunc* that locate and temporalize the event; it is the event that temporalizes the *nunc* and locates the *hic*" (ibid.). The "someone" does not preexist as a subject—we could rather say that the adventure subjectivizes itself, because happening (*l'avvenire*) to someone in a given place is a constitutive part of it.

Émile Benveniste showed that, unlike the terms that refer to a lexical reality, "here" and "now"—like the pronouns "I" and "you"—indicate enunciation. That is, they have meaning only in relation to the instance of discourse that contains them, and ultimately to the speaker who utters it. Just as "I"—the subject—can be defined only in terms of locution and is the one who says "I" in the present instance of discourse, so "here" and "now" are not objectively identifiable; rather, they delimit the spatial and temporal instance coextensive with and contemporary to the instance of discourse that contains "I."

We then understand why the event is also always an event of language and why the adventure is inseparable from the speech that tells it. The being that happens here and now happens to an "I" and, for this reason, is not without relation with language; it is instead defined every time with respect to an instance of enunciation; it is always a "sayable," which as such demands to be said. For this reason, the one who is involved in the event-adventure is involved and summoned in it as a speaking being, and—following the mandatory rules of the Round Table—must try to tell his adventure. The adventure, which has called him into speech, is being told by the speech of the one it has called and does not exist before this speech.

Already in 1908, in his formidable *The Theory of Incorporeals in Ancient Stoicism*, Émile Bréhier drew attention to the incorporeal character of events and their nexus with that incorporeal par excellence which the Stoics referred to as *lecton*, the "sayable" (or as Bréhier prefers to call it, the "expressible"). The sayable is something neither merely linguistic nor merely factual; according to an ancient source, it is in between (*è un medio tra*) thought and the thing, speech and the world. It is not the thing as separated from speech, but the thing insofar as it is said and named; it is not speech as an autonomous sign, but speech in the act of naming and manifesting the thing. In other words, we could also say that it is the thing in its pure sayability, its happening in language. In 1969, resuming Bréhier's ideas in *The Logic of Sense*, Deleuze wrote that "the event is not what happens (the accident), rather it is, in what happens, the pure expressible that signals and awaits us" (Deleuze, 170). In this sense, it is something that, beyond resignation and resentment, must be desired and loved by the one to whom it occurs, because he first and foremost sees in what occurs the adventure that involves him and that he must recognize, in order to live up to it.

It is important to specify that what is at stake in the individual's acceptance of the adventure that happens (*avviene*) to him is not the subject's free choice; it is not a matter of freedom. Desiring the event simply means feeling it as one's own, venturing into it, that is, fully meeting its challenge, but without the need for something like a decision. It is only in this way that the event, which as such does not depend on us, becomes an adventure; it becomes ours, or, rather, we become its subjects.

The Nietzschean doctrine of *amor fati* should be revisited from this perspective. Fate and adventure, Ananke and Tyche, do not coincide. Saying yes to the "most terrible thought," desiring that the event be infinitely repeated is the opposite of an adventure. As chivalric literature shows all too clearly, this is the case not because adventure cannot be repetitive, but because it lacks both the necessity on the side of the object (the event is in itself purely contingent) and the supreme affirmation of the will—which desiring the eternal return primarily desires itself—on the side of the subject. The one who ventures into the event undoubtedly loves, trembles, and is moved—but, even if eventually he is able to find himself, he cannot but lose himself in it, unreservedly and lightheartedly.

Even the Stoics' doctrine according to which one has to desire and gladly accept the event partly betrays the meaning of adventure we are trying to define. As Marcus Aurelius writes,

> There are two reasons why you must be content with what happens to you: first because it was for you it came to pass, for you it was ordered and to you it was related, a thread of destiny stretching back to the most ancient causes; secondly, because that which has come to

each individually is a cause of the welfare and completion and in very truth of the continuance of that which governs the Whole. For the perfect Whole is mutilated if you sever the least part of the contact and continuity alike of its causes as of its members; and you do this, as far as it is in your power, whenever you are dissatisfied with events, and in a measure you are destroying them. (V, 8, 13)

Here, desiring the event means not contrasting or hindering it, and only in this way—by letting it happen—contributing to causing it. But in the end this is a form of impassivity that knows that events, perfect in themselves, are ultimately indifferent, and that only the individual's acceptance and use of them is important. In this way, events are separated from the subject, and the unity of the event and the one to whom it occurs, which constitutes the adventure, is broken. Perceval knows himself and his name only in the adventure to which he fully and restlessly gives himself; Gawain accomplishes his story and destiny only by venturing—against his ferryman's advice—into the enchanted castle and lying in the Marvel Bed.

Starting from the second half of the 1930s, Heidegger's reflection focuses ever more intensely on a word, *Ereignis*, on which all the different strands of his thought seem to converge. The term, which Heidegger tries to trace back to the verb *eignen*, "to appropriate," and the adjective *eigen*, "own," simply means "event" in German. However—as in the case of Hegel's Absolute—what is in question in the event is nothing less than the end of the history of Being, that is, of metaphysics. In *Zur Sache des Denkens* (*On Time and Being*), Heidegger states that if metaphysics is the history of the epochal sendings of Being, which at each turn remains concealed in them, so that only beings appear, then for the thinking "that dwells in the event ... the history of Being comes to an end" (Heidegger, *On Time*, 41). In other words, what comes to pass, or happens, in the event is Being beyond the ontological difference between Being and being, and prior to its epochal destinations. It is a matter of thinking the *Es* in *Es gibt Sein*, "There is/it gives Being."

Yet, decisively, what is in question in the event is not simply Being, but the cobelonging and reciprocal appropriation of Being

EVENT

and man. As Heidegger puts it in *Identity and Difference*, dwelling in the event means in fact "experiencing that appropriation [*Eignen*] in which Being and man appropriate each other." First and foremost, the event is the event of the being together of humanity and Being ("The event appropriates man and Being to their essential togetherness [*Zusammen*]"—Heidegger, *Identity*, 38).

If man does not preexist Being and Being does not preexist man, this means that what is in question in the event is, so to speak, the event of events, that is, the becoming human of man. The living being becomes human—it becomes *Dasein*—at the moment when and to the extent that Being happens to him; the event is, at the same time, anthropogenetic and ontogenetic; it coincides with man's becoming a speaker as well as with the happening of Being to speech and of speech to Being. Heidegger can thus write that language is coessential with the event: "We dwell in the event only insofar as our essence is appropriate to language" (ibid.).

It is therefore possible that the adventure we have been trying to define presents several analogies with the *Ereignis*. Not only are the event and speech given together in the adventure but—as we saw—the latter always demands a subject to whom it happens (*avviene*) and by whom it must be told. Furthermore, the subject does not really preexist the adventure—as if putting it into being depended on him. He instead derives from it, almost as if it were the adventure that subjectivized itself, since happening (*avvenire*) to somebody in a given place is a constitutive part of it. This is why, before embarking upon his adventure,

Perceval does not have a name, and it is only at the end of it that he will know his name is Perceval the Welshman. As is the case with Being and man in the *Ereignis*, in the adventure event and knight are given together, as the two faces of the same reality.

The fact that adventure deals with the becoming human of the living is implicit in *Bisclavret*, one of Marie de France's most beautiful *lais*. The *lai* tells the story of a baron who, each week, after hiding his clothes under a stone, turns into a werewolf (*bisclavret*) for three days and lives in the woods looting and robbing (*Al plus espès de la gaudine / s'i vif de preie e de ravine*—ll. 65-66). His wife, who loves him, becomes suspicious about his absences; she manages to make him confess his secret life and persuades him to reveal to her the place where he hides his clothes—although he knows that should he lose them or be detected in the act of putting them on he would remain a wolf forever. Using an accomplice—who will become her lover—the woman steals the clothes from the hiding place and the baron remains a werewolf until the day when, thanks to an encounter with the king, he manages to retrieve his clothes and become a man again.

The *lai* explicitly calls the transformation of the man into a wolf and of the wolf into a man "adventure." The husband's confession is referred to as *s'aventure li cunta* (l. 61), and it is this "adventure" that terrifies the woman and prompts her to betray him (*de l'aventure s'esfrea*—l. 99). As shown by the special secrecy of the moment in which the man takes off his clothes and then puts them on again—which must happen absolutely without witnesses—what is at stake in the *lai* is the threshold through which the animal becomes a man and man becomes an animal again. Passing this threshold is the adventure of adventures.

In this sense, "adventure" is the most correct translation of *Ereignis*. The latter is thus a genuinely ontological term, which names Being insofar as it happens (is manifested to man and language) and language insofar as it says and reveals Being. For this reason, in chivalric poems it is impossible to distinguish adventure as an event from adventure as a tale; for this reason, encountering the adventure, the knight first and foremost encounters himself and his most deep-seated being. If the event at stake in the adventure is nothing other than anthropogenesis, that is, the moment when—thanks to a transformation whose modalities we cannot know—the living being separates his life from his language only to rearticulate them, this means that, by becoming human, he has devoted himself to an adventure that is still in progress and whose outcome is difficult to predict.

Karl Rosenkranz once acutely observed that the Grail—which he defined as "a sort of symbol"—"becomes the reason for the actions of conscious beings insofar as it has no history of its own, and acquires one only in the relation they have with it" (Rosenkranz, 57). In Chrétien's *Perceval*, there is nothing holy about the Grail; it is only a vessel of precious metal that a damsel holds in her hands and the hero does not pay particular attention to. It is similar to those mysterious objects—such as the Maltese Falcon in John Huston's film—for which the characters are ready to kill or to jeopardize their life, but which eventually turn out to be devoid of any value and meaning. Theologians and poets only subsequently invested the Grail with a religious meaning and identified it with the chalice used during the Last Supper, the same in which Joseph of Arimathea gathered the blood that flowed from the wounds of the crucified Christ.

In this sense, the Grail stands as the perfect cipher of the adventure. The anthropogenetic event has no history of its own and is as such unintelligible; and yet it throws humans into an adventure that still continues to happen (*avvenire*).

5
Elpis

THERE IS HOPE, BUT NOT FOR US.
—FRANZ KAFKA

Every human is caught up in the adventure; for this reason, every human deals with Daimon, Eros, Ananke, and Elpis. They are the faces—or masks—that adventure—*tyche*—presents us with at each turn. When adventure is revealed as a demon, life appears to be marvelous, almost as if an extraneous force supported and led us in every situation and new encounter. However, marvel soon gives way to disillusionment; the demonic disguises itself as a *routinier*; the power—Ariel, Genie, or Muse—that brought life darkens and hides itself, like a swindler who breaks his promises.

Remaining faithful to one's own demon does not in fact mean blindly abandoning oneself to him and being confident that he will in any case lead us to success—that he will make us write the most beautiful poems, if we are poets; that he will grant us happiness and pleasure, if we are sensual human beings. Poetry and happiness are not his gifts; rather, the demon himself is the ultimate gift that happiness and poetry award us at the point where they regenerate us and give us new birth. Like the *Daênâ* of Iranian mysticism, who approaches us after death but whom we have ourselves molded through our good or evil deeds, the demon is the new creature that our works and form of life replace for the named individual we believed ourselves to be—the demon is the anonymous author, the genie to whom we can attribute our works and form of life without envy or jealousy. He is called "genie" not because, as the ancients believed, he generated us, but because, in giving us a new birth, he broke the bond that connected us with our original birth. This means that the moment of parting belongs constitutively to the demon—that, at the moment we meet him, we must separate from ourselves. It is said that that the demon is not a god but a demigod. Yet "demigod" can only mean the potency and possibility, not the actuality, of the divine. Insofar as maintaining a relation with potency is the most arduous undertaking, the demon is something we incessantly lose and to which we must try to remain faithful at all costs. A poetic life is the one that, in every adventure, obstinately maintains itself in relation not with an act but with a potency, not with a god but with a demigod.

The name of the regenerating potency that, beyond us, gives life to the demon is Eros. To love certainly means "to be carried," to abandon oneself to the adventure and the event without reservations or qualms; and yet, in the very act with which we abandon ourselves to love, we know that something in us lags behind and is failing. In the adventure, Eros is the potency that constitutively exceeds it, just as he exceeds and oversteps the one to whom the adventure happens (*avviene*). Love is stronger than the adventure—and this is perhaps the certainty that prompted Dante to exit the magical circle of chivalric poems. But precisely for this reason, in love, we experience at each turn our inability to love and go beyond the adventure and events. Yet, this very inability is the drive that leads us to love. It is as if love were all the more burning and imbued with nostalgia the more our incapacity to love is revealed in it.

The fulfillment of the senses is the "little mystery of death" (as the ancients called sleep) through which we try to cope with our inability to love. In it, love seems almost to be extinguished and bid us farewell—not because of disillusionment and sadness, as the bourgeois preconception has it, but because in fulfillment lovers lose their secret, that is, confess to one another that they have no secret. But precisely in this reciprocal disenchantment of the mystery, they (or better, the demon in them) access a new and more blessed life, which is neither animal nor divine nor human.

In this sense, love is always hopeless, and yet hope belongs only to it. This is the ultimate meaning of the myth of Pandora. The fact that hope, as the final gift, remains in the box means that it does not expect its factual accomplishment in the world—not because it postpones its fulfillment to an invisible beyond but because somehow it has always already been satisfied.

Love hopes because it imagines and imagines because it hopes. What does it hope for? Does it hope to be satisfied? Not really, since hope and the imagination are essentially linked with something unsatisfiable. This is the case not because they do not desire to obtain their object, but because, insofar as it is imagined and hoped for, their desire is always already satisfied. Saint Paul's claim that "in hope we were saved" (Romans 8:24) is therefore both correct and incorrect. If the object of hope is that which cannot be satisfied, it is only as unsavable—that is, as already saved—that we have hoped for salvation. Just as hope overcomes its satisfaction, so too does it surpass salvation (and love).

BIBLIOGRAPHY

Becker, Oskar. "Von der Hinfälligkeit des Schönen und der Abenteurlichkeit der Künstlers." In *Dasein und Dawesen: Gesammelte philosophische Aufsätze*. Pfullingen: Neske, 1963.

Bréhier, Emile. *La Théorie des incorporels dans l'ancien Stoïcisme*. Paris: A. Picard et fils, 1908.

Deleuze, Gilles. *The Logic of Sense*. Trans. M. Lester. New York: Columbia University Press, 1990.

Diano, Carlo. *Forma ed evento: Principii per un'interpretazione del mondo greco*. Venice: Neri Pozza, 1952.

Eberwein, Elena. *Zur Deutung mittelalterlicher Existenz*. Bonn: Röhrscheid, 1933.

Grimm, Jacob. *Frau Âventiure klopft an Beneckes Thür*. Berlin: Besser, 1842.

Hegel, Georg Wilhelm Friedrich. *Hegel's Aesthetics: Lectures on Fine Art*. Vol. 1. Trans. T. M. Knox. Oxford: Oxford University Press, 1975.

Heidegger, Martin. *Being and Time*. Trans. J. Macquarrie and E. Robinson. New York: Harper & Row, 1962.

Heidegger, Martin. *Identity and Difference*. Trans. J. Stambaugh. New York: Harper & Row, 1969.

Heidegger, Martin. *On Time and Being*. Trans. J. Stambaugh. New York: Harper & Row, 1972.

Mertens, Volker. "Frau Âventiure klopft an die Tür." In *Im Wortfeld des Textes*, ed. Gert Dicke et al. Berlin: de Gruyter, 2006.

Ranke, Kurt, et al., eds. *Enzyklopädie des Märchens*. Berlin: de Gruyter, 1977.

Rosenkranz, Karl. *Über den Titurel und Dante's Komödie*. Halle: Verlag von Reincke, 1829.

Simmel, Georg. "The Adventure." In *Simmel on Culture*, ed. D. Frisby and M. Featherstone. Trans. K. Wolff. London: Sage, 1997.

Spitzer, Leo. "Il prologo ai *lais* di Maria di Francia e la poetica medievale." In *Saggi di critica stilistica*, ed. G. Contini. Florence: Sansoni, 1985.

Stolz, Friedrich, and Joseph H. Schmalz. *Lateinische Grammatik*. Munich: C. H. Beck, 1928.

Strohschneider, Peter. "*Âventiure*-Erzählen und *âventiure*-Handeln." In *Im Wortfeld des Textes*, ed. Gert Dicke et al. Berlin: de Gruyter, 2006.